THE GOSPEL OF GOD BOY

The Gospel of God Boy

by

Christopher McCurry

Accents Publishing • Lexington, Kentucky • 2025

Printed in the United States of America

Accents Publishing
Editor: Katerina Stoykova
Cover Image: Sigrid Thaler

Library of Congress Control Number:
ISBN: 978-1-961127-09-8
First Edition

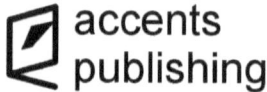

Accents Publishing is an independent press for brilliant voices. For a catalog of current and upcoming titles, please visit us on the Web at

www.accents-publishing.com

CONTENTS

I dedicate this book to my mom, Vicki McCurry, who is still waiting patiently for me to write a poem with "only good stuff."

And Cain said unto the Lord, My punishment is greater than I can bear.

—Genesis 4:13, KJV

3 & 5

The first time I try
in a grocery store

parking lot
while momma

buys a week's
worth of eggs

and bread. I clamp
your nose and seal

your lips.
What panic

in your eyes.
When you stop

breathing
brother I touch

your chest
press my ear

to your heart.
It's enough

to hear
your body

crashing
through itself,

even if your stupid mouth
hangs open and you never

would cry and you
would never die.

Genesis

WHY I CAN'T TAKE MY MOTHER OUT TO DINNER

She's got a flat tire. She's got a dead battery. She thought by now I would have wondered why she hadn't shown up, been worried. I failed to tell her we would be eating in a food court. She expected a server. She wants to know what it means to be grass finished. How could she have known that she needed to order cheese. She doesn't think the meat is well-done enough. There's too much salt in my soup. My daughter's hair has too many tangles. She doesn't get why I never check on her. She asks why I never like any of her posts. Why nothing can be shared to my wall.

WHY I CAN'T BRING MY GIRLFRIEND TO MEET MY MOM

It's not the framed photo of me in a speedo. Not the size of
the bedroom my brother and I shared in the back of the house.
It's not even the stacks of shit she buys for no reason other than
there's an emptiness in her home she doesn't know how to fill.
It's not the drive or the time or the questions she will ask—
the questions all mothers ask: how'd you meet? Why am I
just now learning about this? Isn't he handsome? Don't you think
he should keep his hair long? All of that proves how much her loving me
has cost. And my girlfriend would know just how little I've given back.

WHY I CAN'T VISIT MY MOM IN WINTER

I look like my dad. I drive past her house and go visit a friend's mom and her husband. Not the husband who slammed her kid's head into the wall and bought us porn and rented horror movies for us to watch. Not the husband who fucked us up for healthy male relationships. The new husband. He likes Russian literature, making pasta from scratch, and games—billiards and strategy. He's got some secret job at the military base that we always forget is there like we are supposed to. He's loading a trailer when I get there—they are selling their house, moving.

WHY I CAN'T TALK TO MY MOTHER ON THE PHONE

My mother is addicted to sugar. My hugs, my voice. She calls me just to talk about her day and her legs—those bloaty balloons stretched white hot lines down her calf. Somewhere in there a leak has sprung. Walking is hard. She needs her grass mowed. She needs her house clean. She has eight more years until retirement. I can't stand listening to you talk about the Olympics right now, I say to her. You're winning. You've sacrificed your health for me. That medal must weigh a lifetime. To celebrate, I'll answer the phone next time. She'll eat a cake. A whole cake with one small fork and a glass of milk.

WHY I CAN'T DREAM ABOUT MY MOTHER

Truthfully, I'm scared she'll be switched-handed in her big plush chair
waiting on the phone to shake with need. The lash of accusation: how
like your father you've become in your silence.

Gospel Part 1

GOD BOY CUTS HIMSELF SHAVING FOR THE FIRST TIME

The razor blade
reeks of torn meat
stinks of origin
the first stone
cracked open with heat.

This world of ours
puckers to a hard kiss.

Let him just be wild with hair.

Let him be the first man

with the first woman
for the first time

a people flowing forth.

GOD BOY THINKS HIS FATHER IS A TREE

By that he means he is big
but he is also leafy and deciduous.

He's a flowering
tree not a fruiting one.

He guesses, if you wanted, you could
pick strips of his bark and slowly crumble it in your hands.

He's been told he looks a bit like him
but only when standing side by side.

Rather unlike a tree he tells God Boy
that he's proud of him and a good man.

So it's a bit confusing, at times, having a father.

GOD BOY DOUBTS HIMSELF BUT JUST FOR A SECOND

He wonders if he is really loved
or if he's simply an ideology reinforced
by shared geography and language.

But then he remembers
he has nearly three hundred followers
and all of them know his name.

GOD BOY ON THE WAY TO WORK

He says let there be birds.
He wants to be understood literally.

He wants the actual birds.

He wants the sky to choke,
the trees to be leafed in feathers.

Is this a plague, he wonders.
Should I make some stipulations?

Should I let one speak, but only
just once? In what language?

In emojis so there will be some
provocative and damning translations.

He cranks up the radio. He runs
a red light. A bit of recklessness

is just what he needs before
punching the clock.

Prophecies

SNOW DAY

Three hundred and seventy-four students absent and one
of them a snow day. No that's not what I meant to say. One
of them a suicide. A sophomore girl took her own life.
News of her death falls into our laps, trickles down our
phones and computers. This should not be made public
we are told, but how can we not mention what we all can see.
She is drifting across our lives, shuttering us into our day,
me at desk, my students at theirs with hands in their laps learning
as I do, this girl has gone to blizzard.

WHY NOW I DO NOT REFRAIN

If you had seen his face
as I saw it—the recognition
of my face as the placid
mask of authority between
him and what he desires—

you would not have thought,
like I did not think to think,
that this child will go on
to murder another child
in a park with a gun next week.

I've thought about his left arm
since then—how it turned my flesh
to ash as I tried to hold him
back—when I learned that
this would not be contained.

Now I do not refrain from offering
to each new student a chance
to feel another human who's
soft with love. Ignitable. A pile
of rags. You may be the death
of your brother one day soon
but you will have known him first.

TO THE STUDENT WHO SENT ME A VIDEO OF A WOMAN BEING STONED TO DEATH AND ASKED ME TO EXPLAIN

What part of you
hurts the most?

What part is most scared?

How do you think
it would feel

to hold it
in your hand

and sling it
at something soft?

TO THE STUDENT ON TOP OF THE PARKING GARAGE

So you've made a stage just for you
and below is an audience of faces.

One a clock. One your mother's closet.
One a womb drying on a rock.

What can you do but jump now that the pulley
is rigged for flight.

The night sky is red and blue and
a couple on a date stops to watch.

You can't see their mouths but you think
inside his there is an egg, hers a tiny hammer.

IN THE BOYS BATHROOM

A student tells me he's putting people in boxes.

Like my brother, he says. The best there ever was.

At what I ask.

At putting people in boxes.

And you want to be like him?

Better, he says.

His piss comes quick and he leaves.

Gospel Part 2

GOD BOY ON COMPENSATION

If you would believe it, he makes fifty thousand
sea shells per minute. No one knows how he survives
on bologna strings alone. Elasticity, however slight,
is the currency of those without much choice. He is rich
in avocado trees. There's much more
womb making each day so it seems
pointless to haggle over it now.

GOD BOY GETS A CHECKUP

When the doctor listens
to his heart
she hears in there
a man walking
from room to room,
cleaning up,
moving furniture,
taking down photos
and hanging new ones
in their place.

I get tired easily,
he explains as her
hand explores
his stomach.

You should eat less
fruit, she tells him.

The man in his heart
lies on the floor
in the kitchen
now that no one
is listening.

He taps his head
on the tile.

Do you feel depressed?

Anxious sometimes.

What does it feel like?

Like I haven't been
breathing and have

to remind myself
how it's supposed
to be done again.

Does it happen when
you are around people?

Mostly when alone.

How is your social life?

The man in God Boy's heart
raises his fist, flips
up his middle finger.

It's okay, I guess.

She wants to know
how many times
a week he does
certain activities:

gives someone a hug
talks to his mom
walks outside barefoot
drinks directly from the tap
thinks about his death positively
rubs his shins
air dries after a shower

Approximations are the best he can do.

I'd like to take another listen. She asks more than tells.

God Boy knows it's not the best time for the man in his heart,
but he raises his shirt once more. The doctor finds the man
singing. It would be beautiful, if he wasn't so bad at it.

GOD BOY GETS A LESSON FROM HIS POPS

There's a trick to everything.
Sometimes you have to practice

brutality. God Boy half listens.
He's watched a YouTube video.

All the parts disassemble and
reassemble easily with a little lube.

Get you a woman like a tornado
his Pops says. *Make sure she calls*

you warrior and answers to baby.
A name should release or bind.

His Pops points his finger: *breaking bar,*
cilantro, dog, torque, son. But God Boy

has been busy with his own naming.
The other a day a bee licked the salt

from his arm for an hour. His dead
friend keeps asking to bum a ride

even though he knows better.
What do you say to someone who

believes in you, he once asked his Pops.
I would call that person a fool, he said.

GOD BOY FALLS IN LOVE

What did you expect?
He'd see
a woman
hula hooping
and not know
that's what
he wanted
to say
when
he gave
Saturn its rings?

Apocrypha

A BLESSING

The Storm God took
a mortal man as lover.

By all accounts he was
average. Nothing exceptional.

He liked to count, to catalog,
collect. He inventoried

every part of her, each ridge
of her teeth, all the folds

of her flesh. It took his
whole life to number

the drops of her from one single
surprise summer rainstorm.

He liked to say she must have
known the exact moment

she had slipped from his mind.
So if you are at the park

on an otherwise perfectly
sunny day, no chance of rain

when a drop lands on your back
runs down your hand, then more

spit and splatter until you have
to seek shelter or get soaked,

it's a blessing for your love
life, a reminder to think

of all the parts of your lover
and strive to know them all.

IT'S RAINING THIS WEEK

And has been raining
for some weeks now.

Not every day, not
all day long. Just

consistently enough
to remind me of you

agreeing with me.
Sometimes the world

feels made for us. But
you make the world.

Storm God, Bringer of
Rain, your sadness soaks

the earth, seeps into
the dirt, the crawl spaces,

floods garages, picks
up houses and breaks

them into debris. Sweeps
what's left out to sea.

No one ever thinks
to ask a god how it feels

to bury her father. Would
you believe there's

sunshine and thunder on
the same day, that gutters

choke they're so full.
And the anger, the rage,

like a baseball bat shattering
pretty white teeth. It
sounds like glass, like cold

hard water pelting a metal
roof. We are fools.

We worship a malefic god.
She asks us for love

and we give her a world
full of grief.

THE BRINGER OF RAIN MAKES A HOUSE CALL

Tapping softly on the window
on a chilly May morning—
a comfort, a lulling into safety.
People worship her persistence.
By late afternoon, she hasn't let up.
Creek swollen and greedy runs through the yard
and still she storms. She's aware that merciful gods
are not remembered for long. She drowns pets, rips out
homes. She hears their prayers and doesn't care—they should
have known better than to touch what was always hers to wet.

Gospel Part 3

GOD BOY HAS A DAUGHTER

half grown she springs
from the rolled-down
window of his F-350.

Goddess of what grows
and changes. Of sitting
and waiting. She listens

to her grandfather
while he resurrects
a sixty-year-old

International backhoe.
He tells her how tough
the engines are, how time

has worn out the hoses.
It coughs its black cough
and spews hydraulic fluid

all over the ground. She
finds God Boy trimming
the trees along the fence.

The limbs are bleeding.
In the garden she writes
a story about a woman

who listens to her father's
father creating life. There's
dirt smeared on the page.

Her grandfather doesn't
do the Facebook or the Tik
Tok or the Instagram.

How many likes do
you get when you post
a garden to the internet?

God Boy knows what he
will have to do, but doesn't
think he'll have the strength.

How do you forsake your daughter,
allow her to sacrifice herself
to the fickleness of followers?

GOD BOY'S SERMON IN THE KITCHEN

The traps in the kitchen caught
all the other mice praying
and pinching themselves.

For three days, the last one slathered its tongue
in creamy peanut butter and the gods
stayed their hands against it.

Each morning he fiddled with the metal clasp
loosening its grip. Each night the mouse ate his fill
and shat along the counter top.

He told himself it was only a matter of time.
Meant he'd like to hide his own hand behind inevitability.
Then, he came home from work one day and there the mouse was:

flattened,
head crowned in gold
or some metal shined to look like gold.

GOD BOY SPENDS 4 DAYS WITHOUT HIS PHONE

So what he worships the fat cow
of his own skin golden with suntan oil.
Father, you're at least a billion miles away.
Petulant? You bet. When he flirts
with death it's your throne he bends
his head toward. And every day
is a new bowing of his spine
to the marbled shrine of your temple.
Father, you have not asked of me
a single thing—or, I mean,
you have not needed from me
a single thing. Ornaments.
Windchimes. Scratch and sniff
stickers. Children's books
with little patches of felt
for your single lazy finger
to fondle. Hot Pockets, man.
Father, for all I know you have a people
fetish like some people have
a balloon fetish. Those were
made to burst, too. *So give me*
a motorized scooter to cruise
down the block on and enough
jewelry to drown myself in
the event of a flood, Father. I'm going
to sparkle for you. Zip around
and tempt your sceptered hand
to snatch me up and put me to work
as symbol of your sovereignty. Father.

GOD BOY FALLS ASLEEP EARLY

When he doesn't respond
to his text messages

he learns people are desperate
to accept silence

as love.

GOD BOY CONSIDERS SELF SACRIFICE

And If I ask you not
to kill my enemies

to spare the rod of death
to save the children from

the rocks and slay me
so your love would be

known throughout the world
in every coffee shop, mall, and school.

Not in the spirit. No, slay me
in the flesh, sing a triumphant

note through your instrument
wet with my blood.

Well? Would you?

Revelations

IT BEGINS

Why is it that
        all that is soft
                is sheared
                        for further use?

All these men in their thick coats carry disaster in them.

Their ears
        turned to hunks
                of shrapnel
                        above the collar.

Here's what they say to one another in the street,
    their eyes skittish:

When the world is too much
                drop the deathball—
                        it will be a labor too.
So, too, the newborn
            caked in the
                  red of her mother.

BAYONETS

When you only
get one shot
to kill your brother

best to have fixed
to the end certain
methods of killing

that never tire
and need only
routine sharpening.

The knife,
it's jaunty-lipped smile,

careful and precise love.

CALVARY

Train a man to hate his brother
to love the sound he makes
like a little trumpet swallowing
its own voice   muted   brassy

But send a workhorse to death
with no way of knowing the blades
of slaughter are not just lightning
in a small valley   reflection
on a plain full of lakes and you have

sent our humanity a death we will
carve into stone to remind us of our
forgetting and remembering and forgetting again.

FLAMETHROWERS

What about skin asks to be kissed?   The melt of it?   The pocket it opens

    for the hot shell   of you.

Should be a rule   unless you've tasted this man's spit

    you can't   douse him   in flame.

A bit of coffee   old tobacco   the air smells of burnt

hair and rubber.   That's your breakfast   in your throat.

You wouldn't know   by looking at him   charred and smoking

    the orange   he had for breakfast   still on his finger tips.

BOW & ARROW

Death can just be accident.

A man will run into his own
slaughter eventually.

Become the reason
for war: not enough for you
after what I want for me.

COLONY COLLAPSE

The furthest of us are lost for good and our
mechanized hearts we play a soft tune.

For whom do we rush to the killing fields of our lives?
It's a sad fact of our existence we ignore:

the sun will not even stand our presence.
It hates us more than we hate ourselves.

In it the limbs thin to a needle and with them
we carry something useful: fire, the H-bomb.

The force of which is equal to forty thousand
grinning faces. Fallout spray of vomit in this

carnival ride. If you could freeze this
frame how many flowers could you find.

I'm asking you to bring me back machete armed
and dangerous as I am caked in the muck

of another's blood and rub the tip of my nose
up the middle of your stomach like skin is newly

discovered wilderness not yet wasted with man.

A Parable of Two Brothers

6 & 8

Already I wear the many heads
      of a trickster god

loose-fitted like a cheap mask
      on fright night.

Monkey me is playful
      when you are sad.

Poke your neck, knuckle your head
      tickle your bottom rib

until you choke. When I'm wolf faced
      green and yellow eyed

my teeth get sharp chewing
      on the bone-rope of your spine.

I swear the bull's broad shoulders are base
      enough for you to jump.

Brother trust your body to this web:
      come to my praying hands.

I want what you want, someone
      to hold so close

we forget ourselves—we become
many, we become more.

8 & 10

A father gives his only
     son to the ground.

He will be nine forever
     somewhere in our minds

in a light blue suit
     and fat red tie

eyes and lips glued
     shut.

We are told that
     it's okay to cry.

This is just a body;
     he is already gone.

This is the first we know
     of our death:

our faces will not be
     our faces

and our father who
     is not our father

will ask us
     to call him so.

12 & 14

Chained in her pen
our dog dies in the flood.

You cry because you love her
and she loved you back.

I don't cry because I hate
the stake, the chain, the dog.

Each one a tether.

Hundreds of water-blackened
leaves stick in the fence.

Their stripped veins
worshipful hands

reaching for the world
jerked away. We hear

on the news that rescue
crews couldn't find

the mother or the child
swept to where we all

eventually follow.

Some bent low
like the grass,

others strung out
like a dog.

13 & 15

You die
a skin

peeling
death.

Your blood
water hoses

from your
neck.

I unhouse
your heart.

Your tongue
a prize

ribbon.

We've come
to hate

each other.
The nightmare

sheds my
body from

myself.

17 & 19

Because I've accepted the misplaced godhead
I cannot see myself. The street light outside

your apartment is rusted dark. Your fist
on my back is a second heartbeat.

The air tonight is a long cloak at first trailing
and then tangled as you pin me to the ground.

Brother, there are better tools than our bodies
for this. Here's a hammer and three nails.

We will make a crown of the gash the ground
gave my forehead. Thank you for not spitting

out the blood. Thank you for reminding me
even a god must contend with a broken rib.

you used to have all these
impossible-to-answer questions

like why angels, why one
who falls and one

who rises from the grave
now you think you know

when I told you my daughter
would be born in seven months

I didn't say we spent a day
thinking about killing her

you know the rest
she was born

she died anyway
I've got some questions

that are impossible to answer
like does my capacity for suffering

explain its necessity
does each death have its own

wilderness of grief unto itself
in the photo we took

she was dead already
she had one breath

give me a heavy stone, brother
I have a body in need of rebirth

25 & 27

You work out
sometimes twice a day.

Say you want all
the body's weakness out.

I think it's so you can lift
our father's casket.

Not by yourself, of course.
I'll be there, like I was

fifteen years before
to carry our father's father

to his grave. Death still
weighs the same, I'm sure.

I could barely hold my
corner up then and not

much has changed.
But you, you've been

lifting weights, sometimes
forty pounds, sometimes more.

33 & 35

Resurrection ain't
shit

if your father's
a god.

36 & 39

We've been arguing over our gods
for hours now at my house.

> Who am I to judge
> your god of slaughter?

> Who am I to laugh
> at your magician god?

> God of certainty.
> God of second chances.

Only your brother who loves
and hates you as a god

must love and hate you—
must love and hate himself.

> Forgive me brother for I have
> worshiped the god of this body,

> he who died and stayed dead.
> You say there is only the living

> god. I say there is the sacrificed.

In the end we agree to return
to the conversation. We hug

and you whisper a blessing. I think
how easily your spine could snap.

It happens
I've spent

my life
preparing

for this.
And still

I can't
lift

our father's
casket alone.

You bear
his weight

as if
refusing

to submit
yourself

to the burden
of a body

as a body
once more.

I know
what you'd

have me do:
say a prayer

of thanks
to ease

his passing
>through

>my slipping grip
the aching

jaw clenched strain
>through the unloosing

>of the chords
strung tight

along my back.
>*Our father*

>*who art in heaven*
hallowed

be
>*thy name.*

52 & 54

What of the body
        made machine?

What of your body
        after the accident

in the hospital bed
        plugged into the wall?

Your wife has asked
        me to kill you.

How could I say this is not
        the pyre

I had in mind
        for you?

I'd have hung you
        on a crucifix.

Executed you
        by sword.

Each stone would have been
        a kiss.

God damn the little drip of water
        given

to sustain you. This should be
        arrowed

with half a century's worth of hating
        how much

of you was me and loving
        how much of me

was you. My brother
       I'm sorry

for this death I've always
       wanted

but never knew how
       to give.

Epilogue

GOD BOY SMELLS LIKE HIS DAD

the sweat on his chest / long after he is gone / cleaning out the garage
/ fiddling with the weed eater on a June day / a paucity that reeks /
coins in a dented coffee can / creek water / cigarillos / engine oil / wet
Rottweiler / sun softened leather / so this is what is meant by bequest

ACKNOWLEDGMENTS

Though I wrote the poems in this book, an immense amount of love, support, and work from my publisher, family, and friends is responsible for the book being in your hands right now.

Thank you to Katerina Stoykova and Dan Klemer at Accents Publishing for believing in my work, the Poetry Gauntlet participants who inspired me for the better part of a decade, the writing community in Lexington and throughout Kentucky for being so talented and cool, and the staff at the Carnegie Center for Literacy and Learning who have always helped bring all of us together.

It's hard to quantify luck, but let's just say I have bucketfuls of the stuff because I get to call Meredith McCurry my wife. I'm so thankful for your love.

Abra and Ecton, thank you for making sure I stay young and hip.

Shout out to the Workhorse team (Broson, Manny, Arwen, and Jon), the book club, and the SCAPA Literary Arts students for being my immediate reading and writing community.

I'm blessed to have two of the best friends a guy could ask for: Derek Glenn and Bobby Howard.

I'm grateful to the editors of *Appalachian Heritage, Diode, Pine Mountain Sand & Gravel, Still: the journal*, and the *Los Angeles Review*, for selecting many of these poems, in slightly different forms, for initial publication.

It's Raining This Week and *3 & 5* were published in the University of Kentucky Press anthology *Troublesome Rising: A Thousand Year Flood in Eastern Kentucky*, edited by Melissa Helton.

Sigrid Thaler, an artist from Italy, created the cover art. Go and check out her art work. It's truly incredible.

ABOUT THE AUTHOR

A high school English teacher, Christopher McCurry was named the 2021 Kentucky High School Teacher of the Year for his work teaching poetry and advocating for equity in Kentucky schools. In 2015, Christopher co-founded Workhorse, a press and community for working writers. The creator of *Yearling, a Poetry Journal*; The Poetry Gauntlet; and the Young Writers Conference, he believes everyone can write and everyone should. When he isn't teaching or writing, Chris is playing disc golf and board games with his family. *The Gospel of God Boy* is his second book of poetry.

www.ingramcontent.com/pod-product-compliance
Lightning Source LLC
Chambersburg PA
CBHW030509130626
46549CB00007B/2905